The
Selfish
Team

Tony Reid

First published in the United Kingdom in 2003 by
ITDA Publishing Limited
28 Main Street, Mixbury, Brackley NN13 5RR

ISBN 0-9544379-0-X

Produced in the United Kingdom by
Wilson Moss Limited, Springfield Road,
Chesham HP5 1PW

Dedicated to Penny & James

Without you, where would I be?

Contents

Foreword

'Team' is a word and a concept recognised by most people yet rarely is it fully understood. My proposition is that teams are comprised of selfish individuals whose motivation to participate in any team is driven by the most basic of human needs - to survive and grow. I hope that this book offers you some new ideas about how teams work and intrigues you enough to read through to the end.

It often seems to me that people who have accepted the mantle of team player and have shared with others the responsibility of bringing about change are deceived. To paraphrase that well-known quotation, they are encouraged to 'ask not what your organisation can do for you but what you can do for your organisation'. I for one do not find it surprising that such one-sided demands lead to immense frustrations - for both the individual and the organisation.

The premise of The Selfish Team is that teams - whatever their constitution - are primarily driven by emotion and, most relevantly, by the emotions and needs of the individuals in the team. My assertion is that teams function most successfully by recognising and using the emotion of selfishness. I believe that human beings will co-operate with each other if co-operation satisfies a personal objective.

My vision of a successful team is one in which the openness of the environment and the supportiveness of the team members towards one another are evidenced by positive behaviours and practical qualities that bring about benefits for everyone - the individual, the team and the organisation.

The Selfish Team is not a simple solution to the teamwork challenge. As with many new ideas, the concept is a recipe for the most powerful team *or* for disaster, depending on how it is introduced, managed and supported. It requires long-term commitment and an investment in behavioural awareness and role-modelling to avoid being undermined by the old enemies of short-termism and immediate results.

I believe it is particularly relevant in turbulent times to challenge established ways. Accepting The Selfish Team approach will require some re-learning and some un-learning, and it is worth thinking about the well-established competence model:

> When we take on something new, we are in a state of *unconscious incompetence* i.e. we don't know what we don't know;
> in the early stages of exploring the new topic or skill, we progress to the stage of *conscious incompetence* i.e. we discover just how much we don't know;
> in the experimentation stage, we develop and apply *conscious competence* i.e. we are careful and deliberate in applying what we know;

and in the final stage of *unconscious competence* we apply the new knowledge, skills or behaviours without conscious thought.

The competence model relies on our ability to create and sustain an environment in which people can learn because at any stage up to unconscious competence we can forget or lose the ability we have developed. Even after we have acquired unconscious competence it is easy to lapse into automatic pilot mode and forget the significance of a learned behaviour or skill - how many of us have become 'lazy' drivers since passing our driving test?

The Selfish Team model recognises that, under pressure, our emotions take over in immediate, powerful and intensely subjective ways. We tend to act first and think afterwards. In our struggle to work rationally and intelligently, our emotions repeatedly make themselves known and it is this that makes us human. This is the challenge of working with other people but, if understood and harnessed, it is this emotional intelligence that helps us accept and value the importance of all styles in a team.

In The Selfish Team environment there is also the need to shift from a high content of *managing* to *leadership.* We need to move from *managing* systems, procedures and resources, via *leading* with charisma and credibility to build loyalty and commitment, to *leadership* as a skill that can be applied by the most appropriate person at a given time.

And how should the success of The Selfish Team be measured?

I believe that it should be measured no differently from any other business investment, i.e. by assessing its impact on the achievement of the organisation's strategy and objectives. What is needed, however, is the ability to measure the value of people as an identifiable asset, and the synergy of people in teams as a distinguishable factor. The accountancy profession has a lot to answer for in only being able to record the cost of people and not their value.

I am a practitioner rather than a theorist - and I do not wear that as either a badge of honour or regret - with skills learned and knowledge gained over the years. This book is partly a reflection on those years.

As with any book that is based upon the passionate beliefs of the author, some readers will identify immediately with my thoughts and experiences while others will challenge them as just another theory.

I discovered the quotation from David Hume's *Treatise of Human Nature* soon after beginning this book and I offer it opposite because it concisely summarises the concept of The Selfish Team and it shows that it is not a novel interpretation of human relationships.

I hope that *my* selfish altruism in writing this book is to *our* mutual benefit. I will, of course, welcome any feedback.

Tony Reid
December 2002

I learn to do service to another, without bearing him any real kindness, because I foresee that he will return my service in expectation of another of the same kind and in order to maintain the same correspondence of good offices with me or others.

And accordingly, after I have served him and he is in possession of the advantage arising from my action, he is induced to perform his part, as foreseeing the consequence of his refusal.

David Hume
A Treatise of Human Nature, 1737

Acknowledgements

The idea of The Selfish Team first surfaced five years ago, prompted by a request from my wife for a development idea for a 'top team' that needed a new stimulus. They seemed to have been through every known team-building activity, role, process, and system, and yet they recognised there was something missing from the way they worked together.

From such beginnings my fascination with how teams function effectively began to grow and it was fostered by friends and colleagues who suggested that the idea should be developed into a book.

I wish to thank all those people who not only gave moral support and offered helpful advice but profferred laughter to help me through the new experience of authorship. I must make special mention of the following individuals who read The Selfish Team in draft form and took time to make helpful and incisive suggestions that I have incorporated into the final text: Chris Warren, Simon Napier-Munn, Janet Tennant, Hester Casey, Charles Silvester and Jacqui Thornton. I am particularly indebted to my son, James for his amazing skill with technology.

My thanks also go to all those who have experienced the concept of The Selfish Team within other programmes that we have designed and delivered. Their feedback was less formal and given with such admirable directness that I began to understand the impact of my own theory.

I am also grateful to past and present senior executives at Inscape Publishing, Inc. for their encouragement and opportunities to expose The Selfish Team to an international audience. My appreciation also goes to my friend and colleague, Jeff Taylor of R C Taylor and Associates, Inc. who has been road-testing The Selfish Team model in the United States and assures me that the concept travels well.

Finally, my greatest thanks go to Penny, my wife and business partner, who has been my editor, contributor, critic, supporter and friend throughout this experience and without whom this book would not have been published.

Tony Reid
December 2002

Chapter 1

We have all seen teams in action - and maybe even participated in some - recognising the triumphs of the successful and sharing the frustrations of the unsuccessful, without understanding the reasons why.

Despite the books and models on team development that have appeared before, none has suggested capitalising on the basic human emotion of self-interest. By that I do not mean self-gratification and intrinsic selfishness. What I mean is an established understanding that self-interest includes indirect reciprocity. It is this co-operation with others that forms the basis of alliances and mutually beneficial treaties.

This book is about teams; real teams that perform, not amorphous groups that are called teams because organisations think the word is somehow motivating. Capturing the elusive difference that turns groups of individuals into successful teams is of potential benefit to us all.

Part of the problem starts with the word "team". It is so familiar to everyone that the real meaning is often lost.

The Shorter Oxford English dictionary defines a team as "a number of persons associated in some joint action" or "a definite number of persons forming a side in a match". Whichever definition you subscribe to, you may feel that neither offers a full explanation. In my view, both identify the "what" but not the "why".

Why have so many people in so many organisations failed to work together to achieve the triumphs of combined action?

Most organisations, through their senior executives, advocate teamwork. However, in many organisations this is used as a euphemism for "get on with what I tell you to do and do it for the good of the cause." 'Teamwork' is a frequently contrived and superficial misnomer, created in the 1970s when 'appearance over substance' was a significant feature of management-speak.

We need to make better decisions about when and how to encourage and use teams. It is critically important, right at the beginning, to be precise about what a team is and what it isn't.

More time than ever is being devoted these days to the composition of teams based on various hypotheses and models. The most common is that of team role theory. Spending more time on the team than on the individuals ignores the crucial factor that makes teams work - the individuals themselves - and the impact that those individuals have on each other.

In reality, a team is a group of individuals who have needs, desires, drives and intelligence. They know that working together successfully requires them to listen to and support the views of others and apply values that contribute to exceptional team performance. By openly supporting the interests and achievements of others, The Selfish Team not only recognises individual performance, but also the corporate performance of the entire team.

The essence of a team is therefore a common commitment to succeed. Without such a focus, groups perform as individuals only, with no collective responsibility for team achievement. Until organisations understand that they are competing with an individual's commitment to their personal needs, teams will not be fully functional.

My argument may surprise you: that teams succeed by being selfish, not selfless. I know that this statement is at odds with current thinking in organisations but let me explain.

It never ceases to amaze me that organisations fail to recognise the power of individual motivation and the impact that it can have on the work environment. Whether we are members of a team at work, in a family, sporting or social environment, our ability to understand what motivates others is vital to our success as human beings.

Being inherently self-interested, we are at times frustrated by the inability of others to understand our own point of view or the cogency of our argument. For example, we feel dissatisfied in meetings with people who seem to spend so much time on things that *we* find irrelevant, inconsequential and unnecessary. Of course, *they* may also be thinking this about us.

I have spent many days of my life in situations that have not given me personal satisfaction. Even more frustrating was that I did not understand why.

This was the start of my own journey of discovery into the effective working of teams, and it helped me understand that personal satisfaction and organisational success are not mutually incompatible. Motivation is an ever-present force in my life as in everybody else's and explains why I am sitting in front of this computer transferring my thoughts into print.

Put simply: unless I understand my motives I will not be able to create, or make the most of, situations that meet my underlying need for fulfilment. Socrates was right when he said "Know Thyself".

Unless we understand the fact that human beings are first and foremost emotional creatures, little progress will be made in any organisation, whether it is a small group of individuals (regarded as a team) or a large conglomerate that works by traditional hierarchical management.

Emotions are the most powerful drivers of human motives - they are our deepest feelings, desires and ambitions - and they are key to our overall well-being. Under pressure, our emotions take over as the innate guide on what to do in any given circumstances. The very nature of human emotion means that its influence on interpersonal relationships is immediate, powerful and intensely subjective.

While we know we *can* be thoughtful and rational, we recognise that this is secondary to the power of emotion. We tend to act first and think afterwards, yet when we do think - and if we think deeply in ways that tap into our underlying beliefs and values - we sense that our reality is, at its worst, motivated by self-interest and need.

The most enduring and comprehensible model of human needs was devised by Abraham Maslow and is worthy of inclusion here. He theorised that the primary influences on an individual's motivations, priorities and behaviours are whatever needs are being experienced at any given moment.

He represented these needs in the form of a five level pyramid (usually referred to as Maslow's Hierarchy) founded on the most basic of human needs - survival - and building up to self-actualisation or fulfilment.

Figure 1: Maslow's Hierarchy of Human Needs

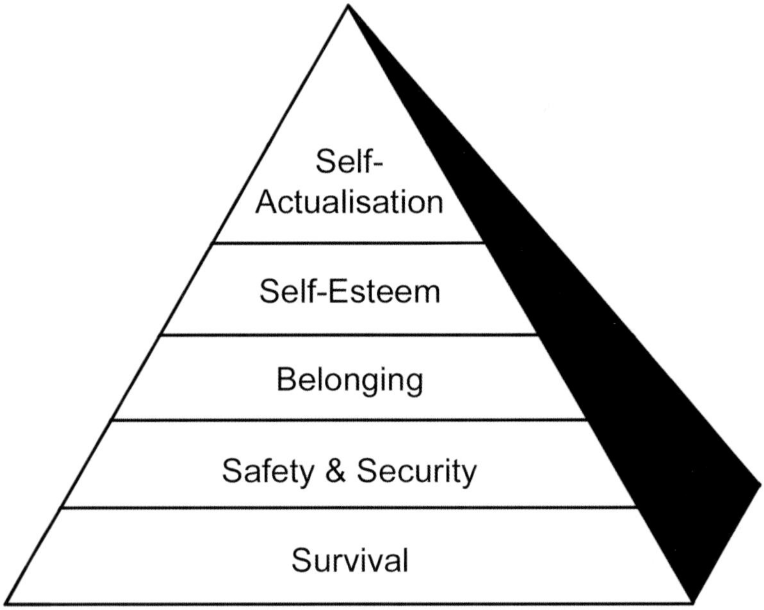

The basic principles of the model include:

- A 'need' is a deficit
- A 'motive' is a 'need' or 'desire' coupled with 'intention'
- Unsatisfied needs are prime sources of motivation
- Partial fulfilment of needs at lower levels are necessary before awareness of and desire to fulfil higher level needs

The theory infers the likelihood of simultaneous and various needs at different levels. This aspect - and the relative intensity and impact of such needs - has much relevance to The Selfish Team model, in particular the need to succeed on one's own terms.

Recent development of the model also suggests that fulfilment of the highest level need (self-actualisation) is a pre-requisite for individuals to consider giving more of themselves to an organisation, a community and, ultimately, to society. This contributes meaningfully to discussions about why individuals cannot be motivated by others but are driven by their own sense of self.

I have deliberately used the word selfish in the context of teams although I consider that humans are instinctively team players. So why does the argument seem so paradoxical?

I believe that human beings will co-operate if co-operation is accompanied by a personal advantage. I will help you defend your territory and help you hunt for food because I realise it is better for me if we work together to achieve our objectives of survival and security.

It is out of self-interest that we offer to stand together rather than alone, and if we recognise such individual rationale we have a better chance of working *with* rather than *against* individual needs.

When invited into the team arena, many people feel blackmailed into team behaviour, bludgeoned into believing that as employees they have a daily duty to suppress their own needs in pursuit of organisational demands. If anything, it is not just blackmail but *emotional* blackmail based on the 'we employ you therefore you owe us' premise. For many of us that is totally unacceptable because it is morally flawed. It is also the most unproductive, inefficient and ineffective way of running teams.

Whatever roles we presently play, we recognise that our range of knowledge and skill is not sufficient to get the job done and our need for more means that we have to reach out to others in the organisation and acquire their expertise to complete the knowledge/skill matrix. It becomes "the whole is the sum of its parts" with the proviso that it can only be *greater* if the individual parts can work well together.

It is at this level that individuals must understand the needs of others in the group - and not just on a superficial level. There is an important requirement to get beneath the surface to expose the truth about what each individual requires as a price for joining the team.

Success in teams requires a permanent change in behaviour – an emotional skill that requires the individual to be absolutely truthful about where they are coming from. In consequence, starting to recognise the difference between self and others means accepting that different is different, not wrong, then valuing and celebrating that difference.

The Selfish Team instils this new principle of behavioural change in all members by exploring individuals' preferred behavioural needs and establishing the ground rules of interpersonal relationships based on honesty. It requires a new perspective on personal development as there is only so much that one can do in a training environment. The change in ingrained behavioural habits must be carried into one's personal life in the journey to create new habits of self-awareness, empathy, communication and co-operation.

The implication is clear – this has to be a life changing decision. If you want to influence anyone to a course of action, the benefit to the individual who is considering the change has to be manifestly clear and unambiguous. Then and only then will the decision to move forward be taken willingly. My premise is that teams are primarily driven by the emotions and needs of the individuals in the team. My assertion is that teams function most successfully by recognising and using the emotion of selfishness.

Chapter 2

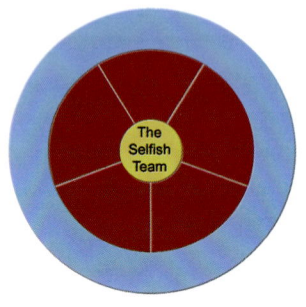

There are many examples in the animal kingdom to support the assertion that each individual plays its part in the survival and propagation of the species. Ants and bees sacrifice themselves to protect the rest of their species in *what appear to humans* to be pre-programmed acts of martyrdom. Human beings differ only in their ability to rationalise their actions: *Cogito ergo sum - I think therefore I am.*

We learned that to survive we had to band together to gather food: ten men hunting a fast-moving, powerful animal will always have more chance of success than one on his own. Our decision to throw in our lot with others was based not on altruism, but on a consciously selfish need to survive, grow and develop.

So it is with modern management teams. Every organisation is populated and run by teams - the Executive Board, management and supervisory teams, and the frontline workforce. Individuals will, subject to their own personal motives, agree to work with others to achieve an objective, be it corporate or functional.

If we are to stop the inefficacy of teams in organisations, we have to believe in the virtue of constructive self-interest that *can* make teams work. As an example of how difficult this process is, let me offer you an example.

I was asked to run a three-day team development workshop for an IT department within a large multinational organisation. The reason given was that as a global team there was little evidence of productive working relationships in their provision of sales process systems for the international sales offices.

Each team member had their own territorial responsibilities, with priorities that were decided by respective directors. On my introduction to the team of fifteen on the first day it became quickly apparent that although there was a reasonably friendly relationship between individuals it was based primarily on 'having been around together for a long time'.

The real eye opener was that, because of pressure from directors, they were entirely task focused - during refreshment breaks they were exchanging information on the number and content of emails each had received that day. I have never seen so many attendees at a workshop spend so much time using mobile telephones or responding to emails. There was no collaboration and co-operation – there was no time for it. The only common bond seemed to come from the expression: 'We always over-promise, under-deliver and bring it in over budget'.

So instead of the team understanding the vision of a

united global team it was in danger of disintegrating under unacceptable and unchallenged pressure.

Those people were not unintelligent and many were bright, perceptive and conscientious but in such an environment, they were cynical about team development. As all groups do, they had established a set of norms, both tacit - as in how they interacted and what behaviours were acceptable - and expressed - as in procedures and rules. They had created a group culture but it had nothing to do with being a team.

Many organisations are, I believe, suffering problems in teams because of a primarily top-down approach that excludes others from the decision-making process. The most frustrating and destructive element of such a practice is the awful waste of bright, willing - and often, expensive - people who are ignored and sometimes ridiculed for their innovative and creative ideas, enthusiasm and commitment - all prematurely relegated to the organisational scrap heap.

I too have played my part in this organisational conspiracy as a former director of a large multi-billion pound international organisation. I believed that strategy, policy and direction were top-down decisions which, by their very nature, left little room for individuality, and were more about directives.

It is interesting to reflect on how surprised my colleagues and I were at the time by the lack of enthusi-asm of those thousands of employees who took the corporate missives as passing fads that would in time be replaced by familiar sounding others.

I contend that teams do not fail because of lack of support or good intentions. They fail because of the inherent lack of trust created by the actions and behaviours of those above them in the hierarchy whose arrogance implies that the lower down you are, the less you can understand or deal with the complex-ities of a large organisation.

With that kind of culture in place it should not be such a surprise that organisations fail to achieve their cor-porate goals - not just occasionally, but consistently. They do not see that their best resource - people - will succeed if they are allowed to use their skills and knowledge to improve the way the organisation works within a framework of corporate objectives. Some companies *are* realising that there are hidden reserves of talent available to them, but so many others are not.

In contrast, empowered individuals will not only will-ingly co-operate but also promote the environment of trust that is the cornerstone of both personal and cor-porate achievement.

We do not need complicated organisations

What we need are simple organisations doing the right things the right way with the right people committed to a clear philosophy, i.e. it is my responsibility to grow the company through my own efforts and the efforts of my team so that we can secure our existing and future objectives. My selfishness - without losing the essence of driving my motives - must appear as altruism within a team environment because I know that if I do not adapt, we will all bear the consequences.

There are, no doubt, many well-written and researched books on teams and team-building. However, very few have been radical in their approach. I contend that people do not adopt structures, roles or certain types of behaviours just because it says so in a book. They need to see the value in terms of their own selfishness! Not only will they not adopt imposed ideas, but most people will react vehemently against them and while this may not be clearly visible, it is often reserved for future use. Herzberg called it 'remembered hurt'. I have also heard of it leading to 'vicious compliance'.

People <u>do</u> want to be part of a group (see Maslow's Hierarchy of Needs in Chapter 1) and to play their part in the decision-making process, but for the team to benefit, they need to do so on their own terms, not yours.

Understanding your fellow human beings starts with

your recognition of who they are, and not trying to force them to assume roles or subsume their own needs for "the good of the cause". Similarly, you should not be fulfilling *your* needs by getting them to relinquish *theirs*.

The Selfish Team at last offers an explanation of why "win/win" will always be a successful strategy for building healthy relationships. It also emphasises the particularly undervalued skill of listening as a pre-requisite to understanding the motives of individuals in teams.

Teams succeed not only by being different but also by harnessing that difference to build a group of disparate individuals into a cohesive unit. The basic principle is that each team member will offer part of themselves to the other members because they know that in return for this apparently selfless act, they will positively benefit, creating the paradox of "selfish altruism".

My objective is not to offer you processes on how teams handle problems and objectives - there are plenty of valuable methods already published. The Selfish Team is a natural approach based on using awareness of human emotions to support relationships within teams and groups.

The title of this book is a deliberate play on words from the title of Richard Dawkins' book 'The Selfish Gene'. If you take the basic theory at face value - i.e. that human genes are selfish - you would misunderstand the metaphor he employs. In fact, genes do what they are biologically programmed to do. They make no moral or sociological choices.

They just are; they just do.

The 'selfish' metaphor was used to help us understand that genes carry out their function without regard to other functions.

Some people have taken Dawkins' simple title to imply that human selfish behaviour can be substantiated by scientific empiricism, whereas I suggest that consciously selfish or unselfish behaviour is a question of motive. It could be argued, for example, that an individual who behaves selflessly to protect a child from danger is being driven by a selfless concern for the safety of the child. It could also be argued, however, that s/he is actually behaving selfishly to satisfy some personal need.

The Selfish Team is an attempt to recognise that, as human beings, we can *choose* how we behave and how we wish others to behave towards us. In that context, we can begin to understand the mix of individual emotions that exist within a group of people that make up a 'team', and the consequences that organisations have to deal with if they do not accept the basic premise of The Selfish Team: that for relationships to work constructively there is a mutual need to exploit the relationship for the good of each individual. Mutual benefit in Selfish Teams equals win/win, whereas in selfish genes, there is no choice and win/lose may be the pre-programmed outcome.

How many of us have joined a team on the basis of coincidence rather than choice? A case of "You work for so-and-so, therefore you are part of his/her team". I certainly have, not knowing my own team role or responsibilities, nor those of any of the others. I have spent inordinate amounts of time discussing issues in which I was not particularly interested because they had no immediate impact on or consequence for me.

Since then I have realised that I was a member of a group not a team. I have been a member of many groups - sporting, social and work-related. Some you might have been involved in include:

executive boards	voluntary groups	religious groups
project teams	committees	musical groups
focus groups	societies	sports teams
task forces	clubs	families

What possible connection could all these groups have?

The most frequently used and abused definition is that a team is a group of people who have come together to achieve a common goal. You could ascribe such a motive to a bus queue! I realise that this is an extreme example but the emotions engendered in me during my working career were often analogous to those of wishing the bus would arrive so that I could go home!

Over many years, analysts have tried to address the dynamics of teams, focusing primarily on roles and giving titles to those roles. Suffice to say that I never felt comfortable trying to assume a role that was alien. I wanted to be myself and to be excited by the challenge offered by the group - but it had to be on my terms.

I also believed that all the other people in the team were entitled to be members on the basis of 'on their terms'. So at its simplest, 'on my terms' became 'The Selfish Team' on the premise that everyone in a team has to be selfish in order to achieve a fully functioning and effective group of individuals that can be justifiably called a team.

Working together successfully in teams usually involves managing the resources that constitute the team. In most circumstances teams are not selected but are already part of a functional unit. I suggest that there is no need to manage (i.e. control) a team if the individuals within it are 'self-managers'. All that is required is a facilitator to help the team move forward when difficult or contentious issues arise or when extra information and/or additional techniques are required to help the team toward a successful outcome. Even the best of self-managed teams occasionally need to kick-start a task and an objective facilitator may be a necessary catalyst.

The prime example of managed teams is in Japan, and proponents of such organisational formality extol its virtues without taking into account either the cultural differences or the circumstances of Japan's post-war growth. Japanese executives have been quoted as saying "We are going to win and the industrial West is going to lose because for you the essence of management is getting ideas out of the heads of bosses into the heads of labour. For us the core of management is the art of mobilising and putting together the intellectual resources of all employees in the services of the firm".

While I can subscribe to this basic premise I do not accept that abilities and commitment are any less in Western culture. The best way of using the intellectual resource available must be to empower teams to set their own standards of excellence and achievement, not to manage or farm innovation or creativity. People need, more than anything, to feel that they are con-tributing to the wellbeing of an organisation and that their ideas, knowledge and skills are being used in the best ways. Those motives are selfish but the pay-off for the organisation can be of enormous benefit.

B W Tuckman's team maturity model offers a comfort-able supporting explanation that "Groups mature and can, over time, develop into effective teams. Like indi-viduals they have a fairly clearly defined growth cycle." This has been categorised as having successive stages:

> *Forming:* The group is not yet a team but a set of individuals, where members feel ill at ease and tend to take refuge in formality.

> *Storming:* Most groups go through a conflict stage when the preliminary and often false con-sensus on purpose, leadership and other issues, is challenged and re-established.

> *Norming:* The group needs to bring any bar-riers out into the open and identify and discuss ways of overcoming them to establish norms and agreed practices.

> *Performing:* By this stage, the group will have developed into a team and will have recognised each other's strengths and weaknesses.

Adjourning (or Mourning): Often omitted in standard texts, this final stage involves the termination of task behaviours and disengagement from relationships. It is especially important when individuals move on to be a member of a new team to recognise they go through this stage.

Tuckman's model recognises that a process is at work but it does not address the impact of individuals' selfish motives nor the price they are prepared to pay to be part of an effective team.

Theory is one thing, practice is an entirely different matter, and as Freud said, "A group is impulsive, changeable and irritable". In plain English, people are irrational. Some conflict is necessary to avoid issues being ignored or marginalised. Unless addressed, such issues will remain as permanent obstacles to progress and success.

Why is it that so many people have tried to place reasoned theories in front of us to help in the pursuit of the Holy Grail of teamwork? Is it the improbable chasing the impossible?

If you think that building and operating effective teams is difficult, try operating without them! Organisations seem unable to recognise the innate abilities of their people to use all their knowledge, skill and attitudes to create teams on their terms and to accept the responsibility of creating sustainable success. Yet teamwork can be enormously beneficial, with increased productivity and innovation, as well as self-satisfied and motivated team members.

I believe in people, in the possible, and in the corporate ability to drive organisations to levels of achievement that are difficult to accept unless you have seen it happen or have been part of it.

So where do we start?

How about with an individual who, as part of a group, seeks a common identity but finds the transition from 'individual self' into 'group self' difficult. This is because they find the selfish motive extremely strong and hard to subsume for the good of the group. Substituting one's own goals, ambitions, needs and drives in pursuit of imposed ones (usually those of the team leader) is almost too difficult to contemplate. In reality, we have to compromise our needs in return for acceptance.

We are constantly looking for a replacement for family groups that we understand and are such a common experience. In other groups we may try to recreate those memories that pattern and condition our behaviour.

We may never openly admit to our feelings but somehow, unconsciously, we share these with other members of the group and, in doing so, create our persona in the group. We still have to cope with our own anxieties that do not fit in with the wishes, thoughts and emotions of others in the group. To some extent, the truth may remain hidden while we subscribe overtly to the wishes of the team yet harbour our true motives.

My intention is to outline the steps needed to build a team that celebrates selfishness and difference; this sets it apart from all other approaches because its underlying value is based on the reality of individual needs - making a virtue of selfishness.

To support what I have said up to this point, I have developed a model that I call The Selfish Team and that encompasses the elements that need to be in place to allow a team to grow and develop into an effective organisation.

The Selfish Team model is a circular concept that signifies both continuous development and a process that must be applied repeatedly throughout a team's existence. In the succeeding chapters each segment is expanded so that you can see what makes this model such a powerful alternative to current practice.

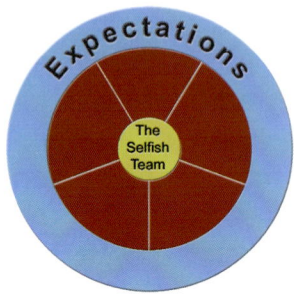

What are the outcomes we expect if we are selected or choose to be part of a team? Are our expectations realistically or unrealistically high? Or are they realistically or unrealistically low? If our expectations are not achieved, will we be able to handle the disappointment? Will our desire to strive for success be proportionately reduced?

When we start looking at The Selfish Team model, we first have to look inside ourselves and acknowledge our expectations. Whatever our individual choice, the impact on "the team" will have a deep and lasting effect.

I am always reminded of the jazz classic sung by Peggy Lee "Is that all there is?". The song uses examples of situations - going to the fairground as a young child full of excitement and anticipation, or falling in love when expectations were so high - and how the reality never quite lives up to our dreams. The refrain of the song "Is that all there is?" is an apposite indictment of the human longing for 'the best' - so lodged in our mind that we are always potentially heading for disappointment.

The Selfish Team is about our working environment. We have all suffered from transitory experiences of disappointment - in our optimism for our business, our potential customers' desire to use our expertise, our lack of growth and development and many others. For human beings, it is part of life. We have the ability to think and dream before situations develop in ways that are not always rational but are usually based on aspirations, needs, desires - in fact, our expectations.

The model of The Selfish Team takes these expectations into account and suggests behavioural-based interventions as a way of circumventing these recurring disappointments.

Being self-interested, we take disappointed expectations personally - we can do little else. We wanted something to happen and it did not. We are disappointed with the idea of what could have been and the feelings of anticipation that went with it - that tingling feeling of fulfilment in a relationship or the exultation of a successful conclusion to an idea, sale or proposal. We can even experience those feelings of excitement in advance *as if they really happened*.

As individuals we can recognise these experiences and the impact they have on us, but in a team environment these expectations are magnified by the number of individuals in the team.

So how should we address a sensation that has, in the past, never been taken into account?

Expectation in its crudest form is the anticipation of a future event, and usually with a positive outcome (hence the disappointment if not fulfilled). It can also be a negative outcome expectation as instanced by "It will never work" often compounded by "I told you so". Difficulties arise in sustaining a team that holds many different and personal expectations of the eventual outcomes of the team's performance.

Given that people in teams have often come together more by coincidence than design, it is difficult to assess the possibility of triumph because each and every member of the team has his/her own level of expectation, whether it is of success or failure. I believe that individual expectations must be taken into consideration when creating a team or working with an existing and established team.

Expectation implies possibilities and those possibilities are the life-blood of those who are to work together. Expectations are the affirmations of success but only if everyone in the team believes that the future offers them something for themselves, i.e. aspirations, development, reward or enjoyment. Expectations can and must be the focus of the future and the driving force that capitalises on the individual's desire to succeed.

Unfortunately, individuals find it hard to control their own expectations and experience both the joys of achievement and the disappointments of failure. This cycle of expectation followed by achievement or disappointment follows us throughout our lives. We have great difficulty breaking out of these self-deceptions. Like behavioural habits, our expectations have often been formed in our early lives and are good for us when they offer hope for the future. Even when we have been disappointed many times, we still cling on until the next time, retaining that optimism for a better and more fulfilling outcome.

In a team situation we have to be ready to subsume some of our personal expectations and agree with our team colleagues the realistic possibility of achieving theirs. This foresight makes particular demands on our integrity and honesty that we will examine in the various stages of the model.

In building mutually beneficial, win/win environments, some flexibility will usually be necessary. The Selfish Team allows that there can be a positive balance of expectations within a team that both fulfils everyone's needs and stretches us individually.

I find expectation a motivating force in my life, filling me with excitement and energy. So much so that when I look forward to a programme I am running, it deprives me of sleep. When I am trying to sleep the night before the programme begins, my brain continues to fire on all cylinders, covering different aspects of how the days ahead will go. I do not know if it is just adrenalin or my expectation of a successful day and my need to do an outstanding job. I see this as a positive force - realistic yet challenging - and I have rationalised that my chances of being disappointed have been minimised because I have prepared well for the probable outcomes.

Because we are emotional animals, we need a way of analysing expectations before we can begin the realistic journey of becoming a team. The more we wish, especially for the unrealistic, the more difficult becomes the aftermath of failure. The more realistic the expectation, the more accepting we are of failure because its impact is temporary and our ability to change our strategy and tactics is made easier through rationalising the risk before beginning the journey.

In classic 'expectancy' theory, establishing an expectation of success is a major factor in increasing and maintaining motivation. The amount of effort an individual is prepared to put into achieving something is proportional to his/her expectation of the value of the outcome.

Figure 2: Expectancy model

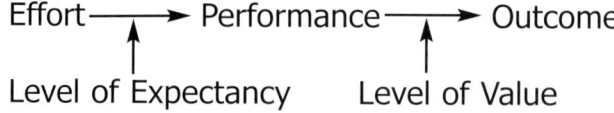

Exaggerating our capabilities and/or underplaying the difficulty of the task will ultimately result in deeper disappointment which will take longer to forget and move on from.   If, however, we regard disappointment as evidence of experience we can " learn by our mistakes" and use the past to divine our future.

The circular construction of the Selfish Team model is especially important when the team composition changes e.g. when new members join or someone leaves. Equally important is that "expectations" surround the model entirely to remind everyone that for each step embarked on, a whole range of expectations must be addressed.

To guide you, I have outlined some logical steps you should cover during your discussions on expectations:

- *Be realistic*
  When you begin your journey, be realistic about your expectations. Try not to be overly optimistic or conceive too many expectations. This does not mean that you undervalue your ability to achieve personal goals, it just means that you have to be more selective in your choice(s).

  Realism - as opposed to optimism - is the guardian of success, not failure, and discussion within the team about its capability, aspirations and skill levels becomes the defender against failure and disappointment. We are all capable of sustaining enduring habits rooted in our past experiences and of ignoring a conscious assessment of the possible. Attainment of realistic expectations should be your goal rather than a wish list of improbabilities that are better left to burn unmourned on the "bonfire of vanities".

- *Use behavioural assessments*
  One of the basic premises of assessing behavioural preferences is that different is different, not wrong. With that in mind, we know that the impact we have on others is the element of teamwork requiring most effort. We have to learn to be adaptable, flexible and understanding of others, willing to give up some of our own expectations for "the good of the cause".

  Remember that giving up something need not be the end but could be the beginning of a whole new world of success. Of course, you can view it as 'deferring' rather than 'giving up', and in maintaining your enthusiasm for a personal goal, come back to it at some time in the future.

  Our comfort levels during change often make

it easier to hang on too long to those expectations with which we are familiar and which, in certain circumstances, make us prone to disappointment.

The challenge we are then faced with is a choice between "is the team worthy of my investment in them?" and "can I consciously reduce my attachment to those expectations that will inhibit progress", or "do I maintain my inflexible attitude?" No wonder teams find it so difficult! Behavioural assessment allows us to assess consciously any inbuilt bias towards specific expectations such as:

- Am I too optimistic?
- Do I fear change too much?
- Do I want to do it my way?
- Does it always have to be perfect?

The consequence of inflexible preferences is that our expectations often fail to materialise. Any 'enduring' behaviours we have also make it difficult for others to consider modifying theirs for win/win outcomes.

By taking more time to assess situations we can 'control' our environment by viewing the likelihood of success in any given situation and using realism to measure what we expect to happen.

- *Remain positive*

    When we adopt a more 'assessing' approach to our expectations, we may feel we are faced with a situation without optimism or life without hope. However, remember that we have only exchanged some expectations for others - some future reward that may be *more* exciting and fulfilling. Our expectations do not disappear forever. We can choose to sacrifice some or all personal expectations in the short term because we have assessed that their chances of success are negligible in a particular situation. Our attitude remains hopeful in the new circumstances and we are open to all possibilities.

    So be positive, embrace change, share in what the new relationships offer you, maintain the new realism while holding on to your desire for success. There will be times when disappointments will still occur - life is like that - but you can take these in your stride and, with clear goals and the help of the team, anything is still possible.

My experience of working with The Selfish Team model is that most people find it difficult to start with a blank piece of paper and express their expectations about situations, other people and the future. Using well-constructed assessment questionnaires provides a focus and a common language.

In the environment of The Selfish Team, unspoken expectations will ensure that whatever else is done to create a collaborative and co-operative working arrangement, there will always be an undercurrent of unmet needs that provide potential - if not actual - obstacles to optimum performance. If individuals know more about how to express what they want and need, they can communicate these more effectively.

In making The Selfish Team model circular I intend to illustrate that it is a continuous process, subject to the normal variables of change. If any part of the team changes, then the process has to begin again.

We have to work with the resources we have available to us, and if we are to use those resources effectively, it is necessary to spend *time* in each other's company to establish our personal reasons for working together, otherwise known as the WIIFM factor - "<u>W</u>hat's <u>I</u>n <u>I</u>t <u>F</u>or <u>M</u>e?".

Time is therefore the start point of the model.

For a team to develop, it has to address many issues. Those that have to be resolved can only be aired and brought to a successful conclusion by spending time together, preferably away from the workplace and in a different environment from normal. Where people in the same team are working in different geographic locations, including the emerging phenomenon of location independent (or home-based) working, the significance of time actually spent in the same place is even more marked.

So what makes a team out of a group? What are the real differences between them? Here are a few:

Groups	Teams
Individuals work independently	Individuals co-operate and don't waste time fighting over territory
Individuals act like hired help	Individuals feel committed to the team
Individuals distrust colleagues because they don't understand their roles and/or objectives	Individuals trust their colleagues because of clearly understood roles and/or contributions
Personal talents aren't used to the full	Individuals apply their personal talents to team objectives
Suggestions aren't encouraged	Individuals express their ideas and opinions
If people disagree, they form opposing sub-groups within the group	People use disagreements constructively to solve problems and move forward
Individuals are cautious about what they say and expect conflict with other members	Individuals try to understand one another's point of view
When conflict arises, people don't know what to do	Individuals welcome conflict as a source of new ideas
Individuals try not to 'rock the boat'. They do what their colleagues do without trying to reach an overriding goal	Individuals agree on the goal they are trying to reach together and feel free to do whatever is necessary to reach it with the understanding of their colleagues

49

If you want a group of people to start thinking as a team, it is unlikely to happen overnight when you consider the baggage the group may collectively and individually be bringing with them. The investment in time for The Selfish Team is probably the greatest you will make but there is no alternative if you want this radical approach to work. My experience suggests that this investment will be repaid with interest.

When writing about the paradox of time, Voltaire said: *"Time. Nothing is longer, since it is the measure of eternity. Nothing is shorter since it is insufficient for the accomplishments of our projects. Nothing is more slow to him that expects; nothing more rapid to him that enjoys. In greatness it extends to infinity; in smallness it is infinitely divisible. All men neglect it; all regret the loss of it; nothing can be done without it. It consigns to oblivion whatever is unworthy of being transmitted to posterity, and it immortalises such actions as are truly great."*

Time is a paradox. We never seem to have enough time, yet we have all the time there is. Especially at work, we never seem to have time to *get* it right but we always find time to *put* it right.

Time, not activity, is the limiting factor. Tough choices must be made and something will often be left out. The problem, then, is not a shortage of time, but how we choose to use the time available. An old Chinese proverb may provide a better insight:

"Beside the noble art of getting things done, there is the noble art of leaving things undone. The wisdom of life consists in the elimination of non-essentials."

The simple solution then is to focus on the important things and ignore the trivial. There is always enough time for the truly important if only we don't spend so much time on the unimportant. However, even here we need to acknowledge that what is important for one person may be trivial for another, and vice versa.

Figure 3: Importance/Urgency Matrix

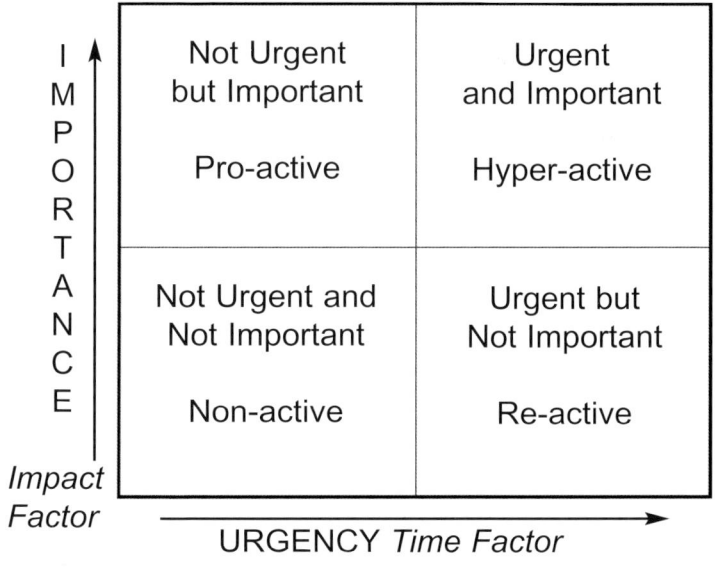

Using the matrix on the previous page to distinguish between urgency (the time factor) and importance (the impact factor) will help to highlight the more obvious imbalances and observable behaviours.

When building a team, the most important issue on which to spend your time is the people that make up your group. However, we usually operate in the mistaken belief that we really do have enough time for everything if only we could organise our time more efficiently. The result is often an attempt to 'hurry up - go faster' in the belief that if we go fast enough, we can get ahead in our activities and actually have time left over.

Of course, it never works and the 'hurry up - go faster' conditions that we have all experienced lead to more mistakes. Who said "More haste, less speed"? Perversely, a knock-on effect is less time for thinking and reflecting. We condemn ourselves to a life of frustration, disillusionment and disappointment.

We <u>must</u> give the right amount of time, not only to begin a process of understanding our own motives for being in the team but also of recognising the difference between ourselves and other team members.

So what do you do with this time? How do you start? How much time should you allow? What do you focus on that will allow you to bring these selfish constituent parts into a dynamic entity that can move forward to the next stage?

In essence, this book is about human values and behaviour inside organisations and our ability to deal successfully with one another. Organisations are not simply buildings, machinery, products and processes. They are populated by people who make things happen. A high percentage of cost incurred by most organisations is spent on paying people. However, it is not uncommon for organisations to ignore this fact totally and to continue to focus most of their attention on the non-human elements, or when they do focus on the human resource, it is on reducing the *cost* of it rather than investing in the *value* of it.

After the first journey around The Selfish Team model - when individuals have found higher comfort levels with each other - there are several assessment instruments that can be introduced to enable team members to develop their skills in using their time together successfully.

Efficient management of time is about recognising the needs, attitudes and environmental preferences of individuals - different behavioural types rely on different approaches to time management to operate effectively.

At this stage, however, I am not recommending any

formal emphasis on 'time management'. This first pass through the 'Time' segment of The Selfish Team model is intended to emphasise the need for team members to spend time together. And again, in my experience, this is something that only forward-thinking organisations are prepared to consider as an investment.

Chapter 6

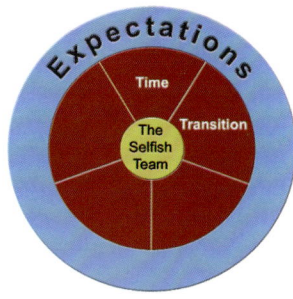

Transition:
Passage, change from one place or state or act or set of circumstances to another. Change from one style to another.

(The Concise Oxford English Dictionary)

In a team context, change is the transition from single state (self) to a corporate state (team) accompanied by the question "How?". Anyone considering making such a change needs to know where s/he is starting from and a useful model of self-awareness is:

> Self concept: what I think I am
> Self esteem: whether I like what I think I am, and what I want to change
> Self efficacy: my belief in my ability to succeed at a specific task or objective

"Who I am and what I want to do in the future" can be a difficult and confusing journey compounded by the uncertainty of others in the team who are attempting to do the same. The process in fact begins with an emotional change of mind: "This is what I was, this is what I want to be."

One of the most useful explanations for understanding the process of change is the work that was developed from Elizabeth Kubler-Ross' ground-breaking work on bereavement. By analogy with loss caused by death, one can identify the phases and sensations of moving from "what was" to "what is" (and ultimately, to what will be") in groups.

Each time I have offered the Transition Curve to people going through change at work, it has proved to be reassuring. To know that it is normal to be numbed by change or to deny its full impact, that there is usually a period of depression - however mild or short-lived - before you turn the corner and let go of the past, is strangely comforting.

Figure 4: The Transition Curve

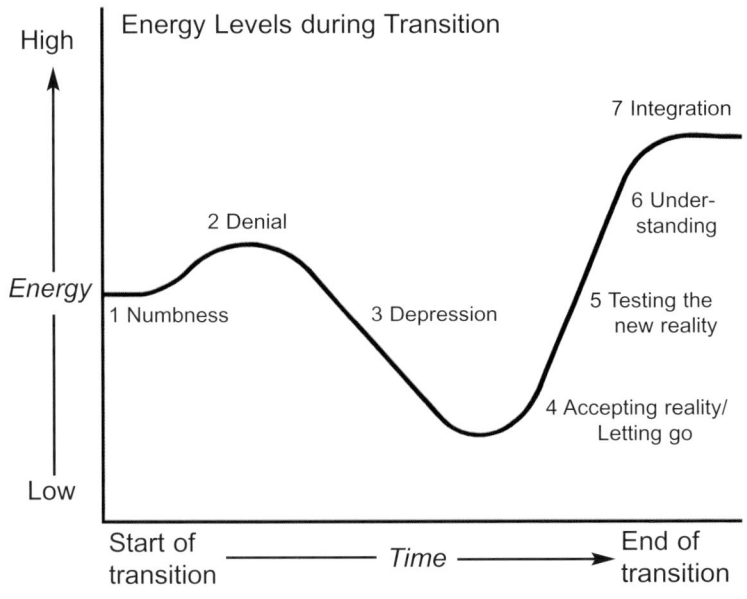

As people review past transitions in this way, they realise they have got through them before and begin to look out for the final upward phase. They can positively test the new environment and rationalise what it means for them before making the decision to integrate the experience into their range of chosen behaviours. They begin to recognise that it is a new beginning whether they want it to be or not.

Changes at work happen all the time, usually imposed rather than agreed and, in consequence, we have little or no control over them. However, the greatest change for us as individuals is the personal journey in which we have to question our motivation, attitude, feelings, beliefs and values in pursuit of new ideals, challenges and achievements.

If the transition cycle is acknowledged, you will enhance the self-development process by integrating appropriate behaviours to cope with change. Different behavioural styles find it naturally easier or more difficult to cope with different phases of the transition cycle. Knowing more about our behavioural preferences in various scenarios is the foundation of our ability to navigate change.

It has been said that what you fear most, you create. In the context of change and transition, it is all too easy to believe that it is possible to avoid dealing with the inevitability of change: things *will* be different. If you choose to stay the same, you are likely to create the very situation you are trying to avoid. *If you keep on doing what you've always been doing, you'll keep on getting what you've always been getting!*

I am not saying that you have to change any of the principles and values that are the cornerstones of your life. It is more about managing the circumstances of your life that require change, whether they are environmental or personal. This in itself will cause a degree of stress and/or doubt about your ability, desire and motivation to begin the journey but it can be helped by a clear understanding of the transition process.

In his published works on Transitions and Managing Transitions, William Bridges offers with insight and clarity, specific guidelines for both people and organisations to navigate change successfully. As he implies: to make the journey there has to be disengagement from past practices, relationships, comfort and security, and replacement by a commitment to making the new journey and creating a focus on required deliverables.

It is important to realise that this process does not require the abandonment of the past. It is necessary to assess the appropriateness of the past in a new context, to discard or integrate *as appropriate in the new environment* the old experiences, skills, behaviours and relationships .

Using teamwork as the catalyst for effective change is probably the most important objective that organisations can address. Innovation, creativity and a common belief in the team's ability to succeed are not, in themselves, sufficient to make change a reality. Making a cohesive unit out of a group of disparate individuals requires a great deal of thought in order to recognise the journey they have to make before they can function as a fully focused team.

Of course a radical approach to teamwork involves risk - some would say high risk. I would say that traditional hierarchical command and control structures do not actually work and are particularly incompetent at dealing with the pace of change that organisations currently face.

Allowing people to turn themselves into teams by acknowledging the transition process as a vehicle to move from single to team state has the potential to produce an energised group of individuals who have found their way. This planned process of transition will cement the team's maturity and secure its long term development as an agent of change.

Understanding the transition cycle offers a framework for successfully making any transition work for you. It offers strategies for handling different situations, the impact of attitudes, feelings and values on decisions you take, the challenges you will face when questioning your old ways of doing things and how to capitalise on change for your benefit.

This is an exciting opportunity for you to explore, experiment, share and learn in your quest for new beginnings. The very concept of The Selfish Team relies on you to accept responsibility for your own transition and to be a supporter, helper, coach and mentor of others in the team as they complete their transitions.

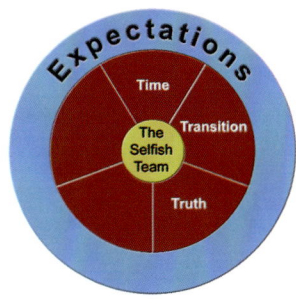

Organisational behaviour is a vast subject and can be perceived by the layman as being overly complicated. My aim is to keep explanations of behaviour simple yet valid. However, they must also be in context with the exploration of self within a group of individuals whose perceptions, although all different, *are the truth as they see it*.

The time that we give to this phase will uncover the real individual, whose motives and motivation toward the team will be revealed - as truth.

Another benefit of this approach is that individuals who explore their own behaviours begin to see that these insights are not restricted to the workplace, but become life skills that can enhance all their relationships.

How then is it possible to uncover the truth and share it with the team? The answer is through an understanding of our human values and the behaviours that reflect them.

For hundreds of years philosophers from all round the world have been fascinated by, and have made strenuous efforts to understand behaviour. They investigated many methods for quantifying and describing what was observed in themselves and others.

It is natural to wonder why we behave so differently from each other. Our fascination is based primarily on self-interest and our view of reality is, as far as we are concerned, the only true reality. Such self-interest lies at the core of our inadequacy in communicating effectively with those whose motives and behaviours differ from ours, but whose perceptions are as valid as our own.

Ancient civilisations attempted to describe human behaviour in ways that are still talked about and, in some cases, still referred to today. Hippocrates, the father of medicine, was writing around 400 BC about the four 'humours' and how an excess of one created a person's temperament - sanguine, phlegmatic, bilious or melancholic.

With Freud, Jung, Adler and others came the modern schools of psychological thought. Freud described the ego, id and super ego; Jung talked about anima and animus, the shadow and enduring archetypes; Adler stressed the importance of early myths and motivations based on interpersonal needs. Later, the behaviourists thought that what people did was directly related to whether the response they got was painful, pleasant or neutral.

Despite the history and subsequent intellectual

'battles' among theorists, interest in human behaviour remains strong. The need for simple effective ways of understanding and communicating about behaviour are greater than ever in an increasingly complex and fast changing world.

For many years now I have been using a model called The Onion to explain and encourage exploration of the relationship between behaviour and its driving forces. Take an onion. Its inner layers are protected by a thicker, outer skin. This is analogous with behaviours that allow us to protect our thoughts, feelings, beliefs and values by choosing how we react to situations, circumstances and people.

In our relationships with others, we do not get below their protective layer except (a) with their permission (they give us information about the layers beneath), or (b) by bruising the outer layer through our own behaviour(s) - either accidentally or deliberately.

Immediately beneath the outer layer are motivation and attitude (see Figure 5 overleaf). These derive from experiences of past behaviour e.g. "in order to keep my job, I have to toe the party line" or "the last time I smiled at that person, s/he smiled back".

Our experiences (the next layer) include and are strongly influenced by conditioning and patterning (e.g. "big boys don't cry", "be polite to your elders").

Figure 5: The Onion Model

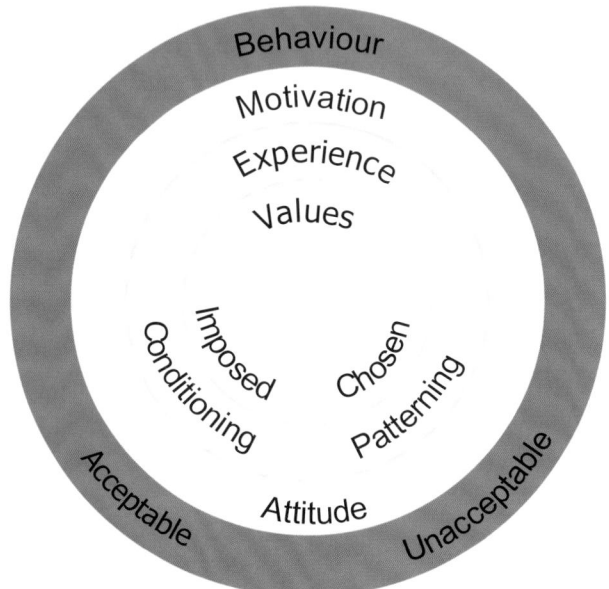

What really causes internal dissonance, however, is when an external situation causes conflict with our values and beliefs. We may react without thinking and then realise we should not have, or we may want to behave in a way that is consistent with our values but experience has shown that we will have to deal with certain consequences.

On considering our personal values, many of us realise that we are still operating on the basis of values imposed by parents or other adult influences from our childhood. It is one of the phases of the 'maturing' process (or 'growing up') that we freely choose our values and beliefs, and some aspects of immaturity can be traced to a gap in this process. We also have to learn that people's values vary enormously and that we have to be as non-judgemental about their values as we do about their behaviour in the initial stages of discovering the truth about each other.

At the core of the onion is our genetic make-up and the ability to make choices for ourselves - and there is an assumption in the model that we have the basic intelligence to do so. Clearly there are circumstances (either physiological or psychological) that prevent some people from controlling their behaviour or making rational choices.

In a perfect world, we would have the time to approach others in ways that offer opportunities to peel away the layers of the onion. But even with time available, it is often difficult to find a way of starting the conversation.

What is needed for The Selfish Team concept is not complex behavioural analysis that requires third party interpretation but a simple and valid self-interpreted approach that provides individuals in teams with an illuminating insight into their own preferred behavioural traits and those of other people.

Behaviour is an appropriate place to begin. In all my

work dealing with interpersonal relationships there has only been one behavioural assessment that meets the criteria of simplicity combined with validity. This profile is based on William Moulton Marston's four factor DISC model of behavioural trait theory.

It assesses the interaction between our behavioural preferences and the environment or situation, whereas most profiles place more emphasis on measuring behavioural type. It is not a predictive model, though it may help identify latent abilities. The DISC model should only be used as a way of explaining current behavioural preferences so that individuals gain a better understanding of themselves and the impact they have on others.

Figure 6: Basic DISC Model

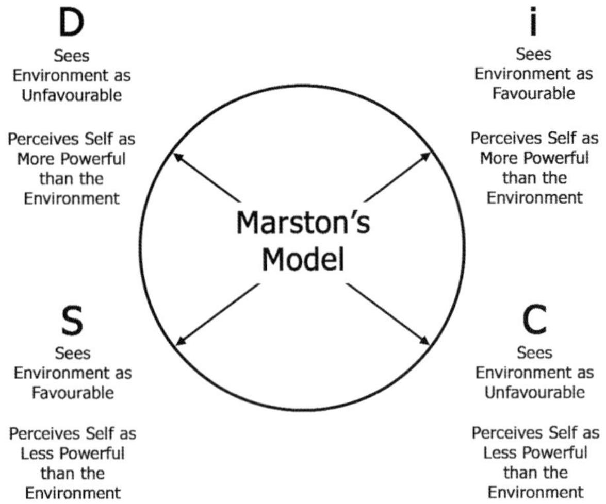

D
Sees
Environment as
Unfavourable

Perceives Self as
More Powerful
than the
Environment

i
Sees
Environment as
Favourable

Perceives Self as
More Powerful
than the
Environment

Marston's
Model

S
Sees
Environment as
Favourable

Perceives Self as
Less Powerful
than the
Environment

C
Sees
Environment as
Unfavourable

Perceives Self as
Less Powerful
than the
Environment

Marston's model is based on two perceptions of the external environment: whether the environment is perceived as favourable or unfavourable, and whether the person perceives him/herself as more or less powerful than the environment. It is worth spending some time expanding on this theory more fully as, in my experience, if the basic premise of the model is clearly understood its usefulness is greatly enhanced.

An important word in connection with Marston's model is the word 'perception'. As modern theorists have concluded, perception of events and circumstances (i.e. perception as truth) is *more* important - in terms of how people react to them - than what those events and circumstances really are or were.

One example illustrates this point: most people respond to fictional accounts in films as though they were real, and laugh or cry as the situation warrants. How easily people overlay their thoughts about a new situation with memories and perceptions of a previous one.

Perception of a situation, of people and of events determines the reaction to them. We know that Marston's model is based on perception of the environment and of self in that environment. In this context, environment refers to everything outside of the individual - that includes other people, events, circumstances and the demands of the situation.

Marston knew, and modern psychological research has confirmed, that how people think about their world forms the basis of how they feel and behave. If you can begin to understand those feelings and why you do what you do, you will have a powerful insight into the impact of behaviour in teams. If you develop that understanding into a respect for difference, you will have the basis of a potent set of skills.

I should emphasise at this point that the behavioural assessment concerns personal preferences rather than the team role preferences. The Selfish Team model is predicated on the belief that individuals have to establish truth as the basis for effective relationships in teams.

The uniqueness of the behavioural assessment I recommend is that it is a self-administered, self-scoring and self-interpreted instrument created from Marston's model. This self-assessment is an ideal way for individuals to explore themselves and their relationships with others, and to take the first steps towards establishing truth within the team.

In the following expanded version of the DISC model, the two primary axes (DC and IS) are re-oriented from the original model. This allows us to see that in some circumstances there are similarities in the D & I behaviours - they are more direct and fast in pace than S & C behaviours - and the 'people' focus of I & S prefer-

a resonance of rightness and fairness in our working relations. I suspect we are still looking while we clock in and out during our working career.

The Selfish Team is a first step in recognising the impact and the power of the self-interested nature of relationships in organisations. Our real needs are based on belonging to something that allows us to be altruistic and to share our knowledge and experience in a constructive and positive way to benefit the whole, as already outlined in Chapter 1.

While it is generally accepted that the whole is greater than the sum of the parts in a team, we must acknowledge each individual in the working of the whole or the team will not function effectively. Recognition of the individual's rights and responsibilities collectively make up a society, not the other way round. If we pay due respect to the individual, giving him or her time to build a truthful relationship with us, then we will be able to say that the whole (team) will be greater, in terms of achievement, than the sum of its parts. This will also be a repeating process when a new member joins the team as a replacement for an existing member or an additional specialist/helper is brought in to aid completion of an objective.

Facing the reality of self-interest in the short term can open our eyes to the long term goal of working in an organisation that values truth and trust. Ultimately, the application of such fundamental principles creates an environment not of selfishness but of sharing and caring, creating in its wake the vision of a brighter future for all teams and individuals.

Many organisations are struggling unnecessarily, and an important element contributing to their difficulties is the neglect of their human resource. The industrialised Western culture still tends to follow FW Taylor's hierarchical model of company structures, ignoring the abilities of the individuals and their capability to think for themselves. Employees have long since learned that their ideas are generally ignored if they do not fit in with the current organisational thinking and so they continue to give a 'fair day's work for a fair day's pay' - but no more than that!

The ability to do the job *as a team* takes considerable individual courage because you are asked to offer your experience, knowledge, skills and specialisms to a group of individuals you may hardly know and who carry their own agendas and needs. Frank and open discourse based on a behaviour needs model will reveal both potential conflict and natural harmony that can be moulded into a constructive climate for the way forward. It implies, however, that individuals have to learn - *and be willing* - to modify their own behaviour to prevent serious misunderstandings and personal animosities from undermining the formation of a real team.

However, it does not always work first time. That is not a fault in the model but an issue for one or more individuals who, for whatever reason, fail to recognise the value of truth in the team equation. If time and effort by other members does not reconcile these differences I have a simple, if brutal, recommendation - change those members who refuse to come along. "One volunteer is worth ten pressed men."

Getting together for the first time is crucial - each individual will be on the look-out for clues from the assembled group that confirm preconceptions of fellow team members. When there is no formally appointed leader, more attention is paid to each other and, unfortunately, judgement based on brief acquaintance is invariably flawed.

So suspend judgement and use behaviour as your guide - in the first instance, look only for your perception of acceptable or unacceptable behaviour. Remember that *your* perception is *your* reality and if you perceive negative or unacceptable behaviour, you should ask yourself the question "Why might s/he be doing that?" because there will *always* be a reason.

Early sessions should concentrate on the seriousness of the task ahead and the consequences of the team's efforts. It is not sufficient to imply success; the effects of possible failure must be taken into account as well - including the consequences on the team's and individual's fortunes. There is little point in expressing a wish for success without stating the reality of failure because, as previously stated, truth is the benchmark of successful teams, requiring courage on the part of team members to accept it.

Although a leader is not vital for the team's performance, attendance by a senior executive is necessary at the early meetings to add credibility to the team's formation and to support the process of empowerment. This will include the financial authority of the business/subsidiary/department, the value to the business of the project about to be embarked on, the support that can be called on, the level of assigned authority (devolved or otherwise), reporting procedure(s), time limits, and many other topics.

The team should also take the opportunity to question some or all of the statements/information offered and assess the honesty of the messenger in the subsequent discussion. By using the 'truth' part of the model, nobody can be in any doubt as to what is required as an outcome, whether it is an increase in productivity, quality or revenue and/or profit, or some other result.

The one overriding principle that distinguishes outstanding teams from also-rans is a personal commitment to each individual's growth and development. This quality is self-perpetuating, leading to a deeper sense of invulnerability, more stretching targets/objectives and a confidence in the inter-dependence fostered by truth.

Having said that teams are more likely to perform above expectation if individuals understand their fellow team members, I do not suggest that this alone is sufficient for success. It must be stated explicitly that members must have relevant skills - be they technical, functional, creative or interpersonal. The issue now is to confront the team with the performance standards required and the necessity for individuals to develop themselves into a skilful cohesive unit. We can assume that most employees have varying degrees of functional and/or technical skills but this is only a starting point.

Finally, as a consequence of the second factor in The Selfish Team model, there is having fun.

I never heard anyone actually say that work cannot be fun but the pressure of work has largely displaced humour as an element of today's workplace.

I cannot explain, nor do I have the statistics to prove it, but having worked with some overly serious teams, I know that - for me - when humour is present, teams seem to excel. It is either a by-product or an essential ingredient of successful teams that individuals have the confidence to enjoy the experience of working with others, and are able to laugh both at themselves and with their colleagues.

Maybe the scales are slowly being removed from the eyes of those in power, revealing the fact that human beings in organisations are the key to success in their search for profitable growth. The obvious corollary of such an argument is that teams work because of our ability to get on with others, and the degree to which we manage ourselves.

Chapter 8

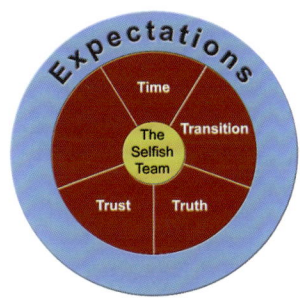

Teams that come together first as a group of individuals have to learn how to behave toward fellow members - by understanding *their* values, motives, emotions and differences. "Teams" are not always specifically or carefully selected for projects but are often formed by coincidence, with people being in a particular place at the right time. Whether specifically selected or not, all team members should work their way through The Selfish Team model and we have now reached the fourth stage: Trust.

Trust is variously defined as straightforwardness, acceptance, reliability or openness, depending on an individual's preferences for task or people orientation and the amount of information needed before making a decision. I will use a sporting analogy as an example of trust.

When I was much younger, I played in a very successful rugby team, so successful that for one season we remained unbeaten and became unofficial national champions. In this team, playing alongside me was another young man who was fit, fast and strong yet he had none of the other natural gifts of a good rugby player in that he could not pass, catch or kick a rugby ball. However, he played every match in this victorious side - why? Well, he had one priceless asset that our team required - he could tackle anything - players, sandbags, brick walls, anything! Nothing evaded him and we knew it, and that is why he played every game. We believed in him, had confidence in him, trusted in and relied on him and we were right to - he never let us down. He gave the team a vital skill that gave us the winning edge. He had all four interpretations of trust working for him.

However, this is not always the case. Sometimes we need to 'iron out' different interpretations of trust to ensure that we have a common perception and expectation of trustworthy behaviour.

The Selfish Team model ascribes to each team member the trustworthiness that all teams require to succeed so that no-one in the team will be perceived as letting his/her fellow members down. Now I know that this might read like trying to turning a sow's ear into a silk purse but my experience leads me to the conclusion that individuals react positively to the trust that is given to them and if a member betrays that trust, the team will be able to decide whether to withdraw membership.

How do teams function when the constituent parts do not play an equal part in the workings and/or workload required to achieve the objective? Put simply, the team - or more importantly those who wish to play by the rules and who accept the responsibility that membership of the team requires of them - refuses to have defectors in the team. This applies equally to original members and to those who subsequently join by volunteering or being appointed. Reciprocity in a team is an obligation by the selfish to the selfish. Each person who subscribes to the selfish motive will fulfil the contract entered into, and will be the recipient of help toward their own objectives and triumphs.

For teams to grow and flourish, there is a need to create a sanctuary - a place where team members find protection and the preservation of the values to which they have acceded and where creative ideas can be explored in a safe environment. It is a place that offers a sense of comfort because like-minded team members express their support with emotional maturity.

The ability to articulate unspoken taboos that are rarely aired in 'normal' situations (such as fears, dislikes and unacceptable behaviours) reveals the true meaning of trust. If you can provoke or solicit feedback as part of the ongoing dialogue on all issues that have a direct impact on the task being tackled, you create opportunities for increasing trust.

This element of teamwork takes a degree of courage because exposing the emotional realities of dealing with people in a mature and adult way means accepting that we all have good and bad days. Ignoring this and leaving feelings unexpressed is often a sign of lack of trust in what another may do with the information.

Who has not felt the pressure of emotional lows generated by lack of time, unhelpful colleagues, home problems etc.? Whoever ignores emotion ignores our human fallibilities and our desire for sanctuary - in a safe environment - which is both healthy for us and the organisation and from which something positive will evolve.

I have always found that Johari's Window offers individuals an opportunity to expand on the importance of trust.

The value of the model comes from highlighting

- feedback as a method of realising potential, and decreasing the blind spots we all have about our behaviour and impact on others,

- self-disclosure as a method of increasing awareness of our personal needs and creating an open, honest environment where others will be encouraged to take risks to realise their potential,

- the concept of 'behaviour breeds behaviour'.

For readers who are not familiar with the model, it is usually represented in a simple format like this:

Figure 8: Johari's Window

	Things about me known by me	Things about me not known by me
Things about me known by you	Public	Blind Spot
Things about me not known by you	Private	Potential

The 'Public' window contains information that we know because it is has been freely offered, observed or discovered. The 'Private' space contains information that we choose to keep to ourselves. The 'Blind Spot' contains things that we do not know about ourselves but that are obvious to others, including how we make them feel. In the 'Potential' area are things that are unknown but may be waiting to be discovered. It is also important to recognise that although the model is normally drawn with equal sized panes, this is not the case with most people. Some are very open, some are very self-contained, everyone has blind spots, and we all have untapped potential.

Using the model in a Selfish Team environment is particularly relevant because of the need to tap into the
'potential' that might otherwise lie dormant in a group.
When there is a climate of trust, people will be inclined
to reveal more from their 'private space' and even
admit the 'blind spots'.

Only after the truth and trust barriers have been
bridged do people stop fearing others in the team and
begin to speak openly of their own ideas, doubts and
desired outcomes. We are more comfortable doing
our own jobs and the transition from self-responsibili-
ty to group accountability is agonising but ultimately
rewarding for all.

For most of us, inter-dependence does not come easily; it must be worked at. The only benchmarks we
have as individuals are our own reasons for being a
team member and the benefits that flow to us when
acceptance is achieved.

My experience is that this painful exercise is a pre-requisite to becoming a real team. Seldom in my experience does a group of individuals sit down happily
together and begin to perform at any level of competence without going through this exercise. It takes
time and skill.

If you believe that this sort of self-managed co-operative lacks control and/or leadership, be assured that

peer pressure is the greatest management control that can be exerted. Peer pressure in these circumstances stems from the premise that if the team feels its success is based on absolute individual commitment, then it is a pre-requisite for membership.

Where a team remains together for a sustained period there will be opportunities to develop this concept of trust so that individuals apply their preferences and abilities for the good of the team. When a team is prepared to allow members with specific skills and/or interests to work on their own *but on behalf of the team* it has understood the real meaning of trust.

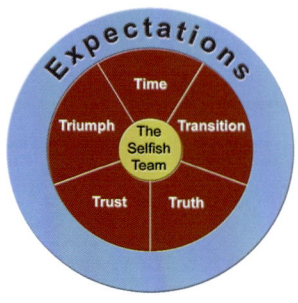

The final stage of The Selfish Team model is Triumph. It follows the four other elements of Time, Transition, Truth, Trust - to reinforce and foster strong team involvement. Triumph means success and is the reward for The Selfish Team's investment in time, commitment and energy.

Human beings in general, and adults in particular, have a desire to succeed, and when they do so, they need to celebrate the triumph. This will not always mean a victory parade. For some, overt recognition is important; for others, an inner feeling of 'a job well done' is sufficient. For all, however, the sense of triumph is the spur to facing the next challenge, to taking the next risk, or to building on the knowledge gained.

When organisations are facing turbulent times, what better way of focusing on the real value of teams than to spread The Selfish Team philosophy throughout the business. If you want to prove it in your organisation, pilot it with one team in a particular area where impact will definitely be recognised.

So is this all just a variation on self-managed teams? To some extent I have to say yes but while the concept of self-managed teams is one that I support, it does not, in my view, go far enough in exposing the elements that really impact on the needs of the individual and the acceptance of *What's In It For Me* for all team members.

Team development is an evolutionary process. It takes time for people to change their working practices and to take full responsibility for their own actions when working with others - I prefer to call them self-led teams.

Putting people into a team and believing it will perform effectively ignores the basic internal forces that drive us. In-depth understanding of ourselves and others is the key to building lasting and productive relations beyond the normal and superficial team building courses that are often cobbled together by senior managers, HR departments or outside consultants. The sort of teams that I am suggesting are a radical departure from the norm, acknowledging the reason for failure in other theories that do not give enough credence to the human factor. Selfish Teams will create and maintain a learning culture that will feed off triumph. Triumph is the experience of success - and the recognition of success by others - that provides reinforcement and motivation.

Teams *can* be the way forward for many organisations but need to be handled sensitively because they offer individuals the chance to change their lives. The Selfish Team releases people from the daily disempowerment inflicted on them by hierarchies that are blinkered by traditional thinking. Nothing has been achieved by maintaining the status quo. No invention or scientific breakthrough was arrived at from thinking the same as everybody else.

Self-led teams that are confident in their knowledge of themselves and their fellow team members can, given the right support, conquer anything. They are of the "right stuff".

- They will recognise the need for change and will drive the company forward.
- They will focus on the important
- They are capable of innovation and creativity
- They understand the challenges that face them
- They understand the fundamental principles of Selfish Teamworking
- They can and will triumph

So what can leaders of departments, subsidiaries or whole organisations do to support change that will aid a team to raise its standards and re-motivate its pride, esteem and sense of importance?

First and most important is developing the team's knowledge and skills levels. A decision by a designated leader to instigate an irrelevant though well-meaning training event, such as a generic team-building day, could have an unintentional effect on the motivation of the team. If, however, the focus of training and development is on the outcome of the team's endeavours it will have the greatest and most lasting impact.

In an honest environment that is unhindered by unnecessary hierarchy, individuals will soon realise what they need to know and how it will help them. Establishing their needs will uncover any gap in their knowledge and skill areas that need addressing and in consequence, the team stays in control of it own destiny. Teams are more likely to claim ownership of development plans if they are involved in the process and can see the potential benefit for themselves.

The closer the training specification matches the needs of the team the better. If possible, the training should be handled within the organisation. Great value is put on training and development by organisations today and a significant amount is carried out outside the organisational environment. In consequence, much learning is wasted following people's return to work.

If the training/learning focus is company specific the use of internal specialists to maintain the focus makes a valuable contribution. The choice of trainer/facilitator should also involve the team, both to reinforce its belief in self-leadership and to demonstrate its ability to exercise financial and project control. Naturally there will be occasions when outside help is required -

primarily when it is outside the technical capabilities of the company. In this situation help can be sought from specialists to source an appropriate supplier.

There is also a case to be made for team members being involved in external (non-company specific) training where there is an opportunity for them to meet others from different businesses (including not-for-profit and government) to gain a wider perspective of how things are done in other organisations.

Knowing what its broad objectives are, the team will quickly establish training needs, especially in those areas that offer the greatest impact for improvement and that enhance their ability to do the job. If the whole team is involved in what training is required then the priority will focus primarily on common needs with further targeting of training for the few.

For a team to achieve and maintain its sense of tri-umph, it will demand a say in its development and growth. The return on this investment will be greater commitment and loyalty - both to the team and to the organisation that empowered it. It transforms a diverse group into a united, focused and loyal team.

Chapter 10

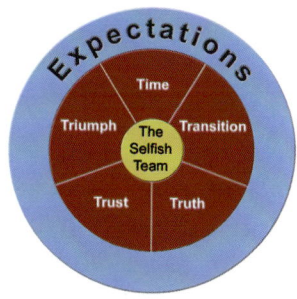

So is your organisation ready to recognise The Selfish Team? Can senior management support such change without directing or interfering?

Inter-dependence is a pre-requisite to the growth and development of The Selfish Team which, by its nature, wishes to work not only in harmony but with the absolute trust of the organisation. Only then can they show how competent they are and, in so doing, return the trust invested in them. This mutually reinforcing relationship between senior management and operational teams can be measured by the contribution teams make to the overall business performance.

The converse of this argument will be plain to see if management restrictions bind the team to a traditional hierarchical culture. Of course in a Selfish Team culture, some 'leaders' will lose a degree of power but they will still have a controlling function outside the team arena, being fully briefed by the team as to their progress and support requirements.

In the past, much effort was put into the choice of team leader while aspects of individual aspirations and expectations within the team were ignored. This has prevented true potential from being achieved. I would prefer Selfish Teams to be regarded as 'self-led' teams, with all members acting as arbiters of the team's development and performance progress.

To the more traditionally-minded supporters of hierarchies, this may sound too much like the inmates running the prison but *leadership* is not restricted to a select few and is not the preserve of the uniquely talented. This approach also serves as a development programme for all team members as one particular skill, i.e. leadership, is not divinely given but can be learned with help and support from within the organisation.

Team leaders have traditionally
- set the ground rules
- decided on team roles
- given out work assignments
- monitored progress
- evaluated individual effectiveness
- taken all the important decisions
- taken the credit and/or the criticism

If these are the normal circumstances found in teams how do you expect individuals in those teams to function at the peak of their potential? *Leading* and *leadership* are different things.

The most valuable step that leaders can take to subscribe to the concept of *leadership* and revitalise organisations is to involve employees in changing outdated and outmoded practices. They must trust individuals and teams formed to be change agents by giving them leeway to perform and achieve, and supporting them with practical help when required.

The key to creating the trust required will always be the behaviour of the most senior staff, with change seen to be coming from the top not just with supportive words but in practical actions. This requires investing time, energy and financial resources where and when required. Only then will culture shock pay off. Evolution will take too long - revolution is necessary to match the increasing rate of change we are facing in many social and business situations.

Committed leaders in teams have to communicate a clear focus on where the company is moving, and that the performance of teams is the best and most fulfilling way of getting there. When decisions are taken at this level, the focus must be on the performance expected of the team whether it is concentrating on production, marketing, sales, customer service or any other part of the business. If a team is the best method of achieving the objective then clear unambiguous goals have to be set.

Where The Selfish Team approach challenges the commonly accepted roles of leaders and team members is in the critical aspect of involvement - in team structure, team culture, team decisions, team objectives (providing they are in line with the organisational business goals) and team achievements.

I have seen many organisations create teams because "we believe in teams". They offer no opportunity for the team to challenge the status quo or to have the responsibility to change current practices or to add value to performance and outcomes. The team remit has to be broadly drawn, focusing on unlocking enhanced performance potential for the organisation. The problems that the team members identify - knowing what the performance issues are - are their responsibility. Their overriding contribution to success is to bring their knowledge, attitude and skills to bear in resolving the problems.

It is becoming increasingly clear that teams are a force to be reckoned with in organisations and are the cornerstone of the drive towards sustained organisational performance improvement. More and more teams will be tasked with specific challenges to improve performance. Senior management must realise that teams will only work to and achieve their full potential if their motives, needs and rewards are sufficiently addressed before embarking on the challenging journey that organisations set for them.

Then we come to the leader who may try - some harder than others - not to impose his/her ideas on desired outcomes. However, even when group members speak out, there are implicit or explicit constraints imposed by the leader, or other group members, which individuals must not transgress, especially when there seems to be a consensus.

Nobody wishes to criticise the group if it might lead to argument or polarisation. We seem to prefer to suggest subtly to ourselves that our arguments are not strong enough to merit such an unacceptable outcome.

We require maintenance of our self-esteem, an illusion of equanimity, especially when there are difficult decisions to be made. Hence the myth of the cabinet decision, propounded no doubt by leaders who make a decision knowing that the rest of the cabinet will accept apportioned blame if it is the wrong decision. The corollary of such an argument is that without unity doubts would appear, confidence would be lost in the group's problem-solving ability and the raison d'être for the group being together would disappear.

Usually the group leader and the members support each other in the pursuit of the status quo, playing up to areas of agreement at the expense of openly exploring areas of disagreement that might disrupt the perceived unanimity of the group. The leader comes to the group with his/her status etched in stone and with devolved authority and responsibility. The other members of the group interpret the many facets of the leader's role in their own way.

There may be a sense of invulnerability if the leader has already achieved some personal success organisationally - such as having been promoted or employed in a senior position - and group members may assume that s/he will continue this success, so their reasoning is to stick with a winner.

Group meetings seem to take place in an unreal atmosphere of assumed consensus so no voice of dissent is apparent, no strong alternative view is expressed and no alternative plans are presented to support a different approach. I do not blame individuals for supporting such group torpor because sometimes the environment faced is too strong to put one's head above the parapet. But in not doing so, bad decisions are taken, everyone shares the blame and the leaders maintain their role. The pile of unresolved issues 'under the carpet' grows larger.

How many leaders do you know who openly court dissent among group members? The only time that dissent seems to be encouraged is when it is manifested during critical or creative thinking, and not always then. I am not saying, however, that group decisions will always be right but what I do say is that there is a better chance on a probability basis of groups being right or - at worst - making honest mistakes from which to learn.

Groups have to keep their feet on the ground and struggle constantly to maintain reality. That in itself is difficult when the leader has control of an individual member's future and is expected to evaluate performance and development within the organisation.

If you are in business, you will have your own examples of what goes on and you may also have seen some good leaders, wary of consensus and willing to expand the boundaries of group thinking. However, even in the brightest organisation the symptoms I have described are usually apparent. The only way to conquer such negative forces is for groups to pursue a policy of absolute openness to all opinion and extract relevant information even when the result can be disagreement rather than compliance.

Always remember the quote from Benjamin Franklin: "When you gather together a group of people for their collective wisdom, you also gather their collective prejudices and hidden agendas". If you do not spend time getting at the truth, prejudices and hidden agendas will prevent the team from performing at anywhere near its potential.

I believe that teams often engender a kind of comfort that is succinctly captured by Nietzche: "They dwell in hell so long, they come to regard it as a garden".

I suggest that there should be no leader but that the

team is helped by a trained facilitator whose responsibility is to guide and support the forward momentum as the team explores and accepts the truth about how and why individuals are prepared to work together.

A facilitative approach deals with issues of self-esteem and gives free rein to the pool of knowledge and skills that team members have accrued over many years in various organisations. It also stops second class thinking about power and authority that was so counterproductive in the late 1990s. The principle behind this approach is represented diagrammatically as follows:

Figure 9: Performance aided by facilitation

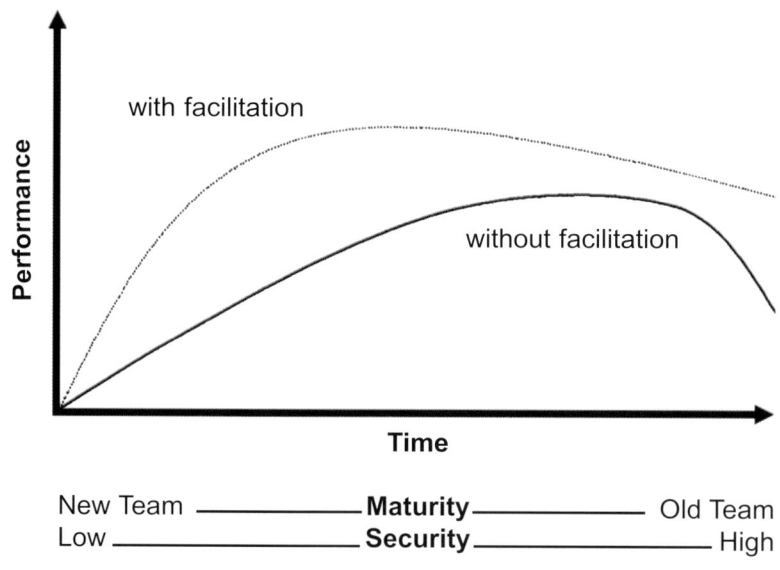

While the team is new and relatively insecure, skilled facilitation can shorten the time it takes to perform effectively. This steepens the learning curve but builds in a facility for reducing the potential negative impact on performance while everyone is learning how to get on with each other and what they are supposed to be doing.

At the other end of the time-frame, and there are no absolutes in this model so the time-frame may be short or long, skilled facilitation is used to challenge the performance of teams that have been used to working together and where performance may be plateauing or decreasing in effectiveness.

The principle is particularly evident in cross-functional teams where there are natural, and often deeply ingrained allegiances, to the teams that individuals have been drawn from. These feelings are usually unspoken but have a major impact on working relationships in the new - and possibly, temporary - team. Reluctant to give up the initially stronger loyalty to the functional team, individuals compromise their membership of the new team.

Consider some of the post-war initiatives taken to improve productivity:
- management by objectives
- total quality management
- quality circles

- statistical process control
- re-engineering
- competences

Most, if not all, were imposed by the people at the top of organisations. Little attention was paid to those skilled in the running of the organisation who knew what worked and what didn't, what could improve productivity, process, quality and what would improve morale and motivation of the workforce.

I am not saying that statistics are not important in the evaluation process but as Dr W. Edwards Deming said 'Applying statistical process control takes discipline and training'. By 'training' he meant for the current employees, because if you want improvements you should develop the people available and let them assume responsibility for the result.

What will not make change happen or increase the self-esteem of employees and their pride in their ability to do the job is bringing in yet more management 'fads'. Continuous improvement starts with, and depends on, the human element and proceeds from there.

Because I promulgate the benefits of self-led teams, it does not mean that I dismiss the reality of organisational life that all teams will be responsible to a "higher authority" (leader/manager). However, I do say that the leader in The Selfish Team situation does far less leading and far more supporting, offering scope, responsibility and authority to the teams for which s/he has set challenging objectives.

Organisational leaders do not have to act as the team's library of good ideas or the arbiter of quality and progress but they do need to be facilitators, offering practical and helpful support when necessary and collaborating fully with the decisions reached by the team. It does not mean that decisions cannot be challenged - that is one of the functions that leaders have to fulfil - a good facilitator/leader will support or challenge at the appropriate time.

At the beginning of the project, the leader/facilitator plays the most important role as a catalyst for action, enthusing the team with a compelling vision of what is required, allowing the team to claim ownership of the task to be faced and supporting commitment to its overall achievement. While the team is active, the leader/facilitator will also act as the defender of the team process to the outside world, to some degree protecting the team from attack or criticism.

A co-operative/supporting role rather than a traditional directing one spells out clearly to team members *their* premier role in the relationship and the degree of autonomy and confidence that is offered. Self-led teams require *less* leading to get the best out of themselves. If the team decides that one person is needed to co-ordinate their efforts then so be it − a leader/facilitator from within the team can be elected to fulfil the role. The more authority that is given to the team, the greater will be the self-esteem of individuals and the group, which in turn will be directly proportional to their anticipation of triumph.

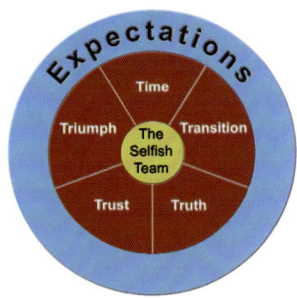

My ideas about teams have been formed over many years and my experience gained in many occupations. What this has taught me is: first, an appreciation of difference and the use of behaviour as a basis for judgement (is it acceptable or unacceptable to me) rather than position, colour, race or any stereotype you care to mention; second, is the ability of people to rise to a challenge, giving so much of themselves in the struggle to prove their worth.

It is a simple philosophy to recognise the talent in everyone and take any opportunity you can to draw it out. The best approach I have found so far is team-work for it not only recognises individual ability but also proves the theory that, time and time again, two heads are better than one. Human beings are social animals and it is the synergy between us that makes human society dynamic. However, there was an element in teams that I found contradictory - the fact that I saw most teams *playing the game of teams*.

We somehow adopt a "we" mentality by subsuming our own personal motives - we become a collective. We erroneously make a trade-off between self and group so that we can sit comfortably within the group without being overly critical or raising too many concerns that might destroy the unity of the surrogate family. It gives us some sense of belonging, knowing our place and the price we are prepared to pay for the privilege of belonging to a prosperous group or a powerful team leader.

However, teams that do not challenge the leader's view or the collective consensus eventually find out why such behaviour is so counter-productive.

I have assumed that people involved in teams have the required level of functional or technical skills to be productive team members. The Selfish Team model - if used correctly - will highlight any deficiency and indicate potential solutions. "The truth will out" should be a constant reminder that whatever your level of competence and contribution, your fellow team members will be your arbiters. In the open environment of The Selfish Team, everyone will be aware of the team's needs and will be part of the solution.

Using a psychometric profile on preferred behavioural preferences opens everyone's mind up to the emotions, attitude and motivation of all the team's members and acts as a focus on the modification required and the commitment expected from all team members.

In life we recognise instinctively what we feel to be true about ourselves and having that confirmed through a profile releases us from the restrictions of how we *should* work together.

We know the truth yet they feed us untruths that with commitment, resources and time, anything is possible. What we actually know is that organisations have hierarchies; hierarchies have politics; and they lead to rivalries. Teams cannot work with unnecessary constraints imposed upon them and it is time for organisations to recognise the reality of Selfish Teams being the natural way of working together.

Truth always seems to me the most natural place to start in any relationship and what flows from that is a confidence that you are seeing the real person not the 'body gloss' or the 'image managed' persona we present for the world to see. However, we are prepared - if the circumstances are right - to remove the mask, peel away the layers of the onion, sufficiently for there to be clear insight of the person behind.

From truth flows trust, i.e. I recognise the values, behaviour and skills of my fellow team members and, knowing the experiences that led to the knowledge, I trust them to do their part in the team. I might take it personally if s/he forgets or ignores the task they have been charged with and the team should decide on the significance of the omission.

If you or your organisation adopts what I have advocated throughout this book, embracing it as a philosophy that encourages team players to reach and stretch to fulfil their capabilities, you will - after a time - have a new culture of involvement and empowerment.

People will work to be part of a radical movement if - *and it is a big if* - the focus of the work is based on Truth and Trust from and to everyone. Managers will not only pass responsibility down to the teams who will willingly accept in a new frame of mind, but they will spend more time outside the confines of the office supporting and encouraging this new way forward. Individual aspirations will grow and set a positive example to the rest of the organisation who have yet to understand the benefits of such working arrangements.

The true test of teamwork is when times are bad because, as with all new ideas, it is easy to discard them and revert to the way things used to be done. To prevent this happening, management at all levels will have to explain what it is trying do, and go on repeating, role modelling and reinforcing for as long as it takes until the philosophy takes hold and becomes 'business as usual'.

Relying on formal internal communication channels is, I think, doomed to failure as it often contributes to the lack of honest communication. If The Selfish Team is to become a guiding principle of "the way we work around here" then the only way of letting people know your intentions is to tell them face to face and to be seen doing what you say you expect from others.

An organisation must serve a purpose and reflect basic values that individuals can identify with (usually encap-sulated in a mission statement). Employees must be able to commit themselves freely to an organisation rather than its officers (the hierarchy) because they feel the intensity and meaningfulness of those values.

This does not mean that substantive business objec-tives are any less important. However, productivity, growth, earnings per share, and the improved man-agement of resources have taken on an overriding importance and we have forgotten how the results are achieved.

In consequence, individuals can and do spend a life-time looking for organisations that can meet their basic human needs and ambitions. These needs do not just cover financial security and material well-being. They include a desire to make an impact in their work envi-ronment by being involved in the decision-making process, to be creative and innovative, and to direct their energies to what they see as a worthwhile pur-pose.

I believe that at least one multinational company has modified its mission statement to acknowledge that by putting its people first, all other business objectives will benefit. It recognises that when people have a sense of self-fulfilment, personal growth and integrity, they will be able - with greater enthusiasm and commitment - to produce the required results.

Self-knowledge and changing your behaviour are not necessarily the answers to becoming a better person. That only comes with a full understanding and acceptance of your values. However, it can be a start, a working catalyst that offers a different way. It has been said that life is lived forward but understood backwards. We need some past experiences to provide reasons for change and the need to adapt for experiences to come.

Some organisations will embrace the idea of Selfish Teams and will see it flourish and grow. Others will approach it on a limited basis probably involving low-powered teams. I ask you: Which will produce the greater impact? If you are serious about Selfish Teams you need to involve as many people as possible from as many functions as possible. Selfish Teams should be working together whenever there is an opportunity to do things better.

Make sure that teams are supported with training and development. Continuous training is a pre-requisite to growth within teams and the investment will be directly proportional to the quality of the team's triumph.

The challenge of The Selfish Team model is to create mutually beneficial team relationships that can work to bring greater organisational improvement and pursue cultural change with real vigour and momentum. It *can* be the vanguard for revolution, giving individuals real opportunities for personal growth and greater self-worth.

A team should set out its own mission and values, agreed and signed off by each team member as their contribution to the health and prosperity of the organisation. Given the cynicism which so often greets the mention of the phrase 'mission statement', I tend to guide people towards creating a 'team contract'. It is helpful for this to be devised during the first stage of The Selfish Team model, and the process benefits from some facilitation.

Typically, team contracts include commitments regarding:

- Acceptable behaviour (including language and timekeeping)
- Openness, honesty and truth (including 'panic buttons')
- Dealing with conflict (including style of challenge)
- Respect and confidentiality
- Deliverables

In my view, this is a more useful development of the

concept of a mission statement and a set of operating values - not as a promulgation of the mission statement fad but as a statement of the rules of engagement and the fundamentals of success.

In The Selfish Team model, it is implicit that there is movement towards higher performance using the unique blend of ideas, actions and decisions. For this to occur, risks have to be taken that may lead to conflict and discomfort among the team members. The team contract clarifies how people are prepared to deal with these.

It is also implicit that The Selfish Team process is continuous. The second time around the model may involve different and deeper considerations of specific aspects of the interpersonal contract. My belief is that the time spent together trying to understand individual motives is time well spent as this will lead to a more open and fruitful appreciation of what everyone wants from continued membership of the team.

The Selfish Team has been designed to change the way that people work together. As most of us know, change initiatives can be complex and painful to execute. Why? Because change is often implemented with a complex planning process that lacks credibility and tends to reinforce people's apprehension about change. What people really want at work is to belong and to perform truly satisfying work that has impact on the organisation's business objectives.

The Selfish Team can be a radical yet gently evolution-ary change process. This would be in distinct contrast to the destabilising effect of imposed and sudden change driven by scarcity of financial resource in the face of competitive, technological or environmental pressures.

The Selfish Team liberates the ability and desire of individuals to take on responsibility for success within organisations, in the firm belief that they are offering their knowledge and skills to the team (or organisa-tion) so that their own needs will be fulfilled. Those organisations that *really* believe 'their people are their greatest asset' will have no hesitation in adopting The Selfish Team model.

Appendix

To realise the full potential of The Selfish Team, I strongly recommend the use of self-assessment to encourage ownership and openness.

As The Selfish Team model is based on the principle of self-interest, I firmly believe that self-assessment - with appropriate facilitation and guidance - is significantly more effective than processes that require third-party interpretation.

Inscape Publishing, Inc. publishes all the behavioural assessments that I recommend and I value the company's commitment to the highest standards of psychometric research. This approach ensures that users of their published resources can be assured of the validity and reliability of the models and associated explanations.

The key assessment is *The Personal Profile System®2800 Series* which can be completed on paper or online. The Personal Profile System® has been independently researched and psychometrically validated which makes it the most reliable DISC-based instrument available. Over 40 million copies have been published and used by people world-wide, and it is now available in an edition that has been specifically validated for use in the UK and Ireland.

Other behavioural assessments can be used during different phases of The Selfish Team, during the first pass or second and subsequent passes. Assessments include:

- Managing Work Expectations•Transforming Attitudes®
- The Personal Listening Profile®
- Transition: The Personal Path Through Change
- Focus Point®
- Coping & Stress Profile®
- Discovering Diversity Profile®
- Innovate with C.A.R.E Profile®
- Time Mastery Profile®
- Dimensions of Leadership Profile®

In addition, I recommend using 360° (multi-source) surveys to confirm that the actions taken during the development of The Selfish Team are having the desired effect. Customised surveys can be designed to elicit feedback on, for example,:

- the team's view of its readiness for any of the phases of The Selfish Team model
- individuals within the team
- the team's effectiveness
- the team's relationships with customers and/or suppliers

All assessments and surveys are available through International Training and Development Associates (details on next page)

The Selfish Team website is at
www.theselfishteam.com

For more information about
The Selfish Team programmes and seminars
Customised programmes and speeches
Conference presentations

contact

International Training and Development Associates
FREEPOST (SCE 10141)
Maidenhead
Berkshire
SL6 3BW
United Kingdom

email: tonyreid@itda.com